TERRITORIES

Sharon Fain

Territories

ISBN: 978-1934828-17-5
Cover Photo by Erich Schoen-Rene

Spire Press
New York, NY 10012

ACKNOWLEDGMENTS

A special thank you to the publications in which these poems first appeared

Atlanta Review: "Holding Her" and "Through the Lens, October"

Crab Orchard Review: "Poison"

Midwest Quarterly: "One Month at Casa Sotovento"

Nimrod: "Screen Saver"

Poetry East: "Chernobyl", "Shrine", and "For Weeks After the Diagnosis"

Southern Humanities Review: "Celibacy"

Southern Poetry Review: "Waiting to Hear About the Biopsy"

Telling the Story Another Way (Pudding House Press Chapbook): "First Day" and "Asilomar Retreat"

Times Ten: An Anthology of Northern California Poets: "Smoke Alarm" (earlier version)

Tor House Foundation Publications: "Demeter in the Suburbs"

CONTENTS

HOLDING HER

Nights in the darkroom, I hoarded
my daughter's gestures,
the way she straddled a picnic bench
or lifted one hand as if to stroke
silk, the softest feathers.
It was her last year at home.
I'd worked to capture everything,
labeled the boxes of negatives—
camping, prom dress, Christmas.

Stirring prints beneath an amber light,
I waited for my girl's face to surface,
faint at first on the soaked paper,
pale as a night-blooming flower.
Time, which to a photographer
is both tool and the thing transcended,
worked against me too. She would go.
Even in that sealed room,
I felt the season turn.

DEMETER IN THE SUBURBS

1.

No one said how hard it would be,
the empty room, last child gone,
that sprawl of moonlight
across a made bed. Midnight, then two a.m.,
then four, walking barefoot,
touching the pillow, just checking.

There must be thousands of women awake,
a demographic of emptiness,
the ones who paid for orthodontics,
packed the school lunches.

They want more than silence,
bend toward flickering computer screens,
moving backward through patterned light.

2.

It wasn't as if a meadow opened,
violence of thrown soil
and uprooted plants, the smoky entrance
to the underworld suddenly there.

It was what we did, she and I,
sitting at the breakfast room table
with lists of questions
commonly found on the S.A.T.
(the opposite of redundant,
the specific gravity of salt)
choosing sheets for the dorm room—
single, extra-long, black
to stand out in the wash.

3.

The letters of admission
were printed to look like diplomas,
bright seal, a ring of Latin, a promise,
the end arriving first.

You might suggest I courted it.
No dark chariot was needed,
no trampled petals.
I worked toward my own loneliness.

4.

And you may raise an eyebrow when I say
sex plays no part in this grief.

We're permissive here,
beneath our laurel trees.

My pain has nothing to do
with how she might use her body
but everything to do
with wanting her bodily presence
reading cookbooks aloud,
eating my lemon chicken.

Hades' crime, I see now,
was not theft or seduction
but making a girl invisible,
face and breath no more than a rumor
drifting up through layers
of granite, shale, sand.

SCREEN SAVER

Heather installed a forest on my hard drive.
Seasons of maples and flame-shaped poplars
roll by after I stop typing. Soft green
or black against snow, trees keep me company,
come when nothing else will.

Hours spent in my workroom thinking
about the body. Twice mine opened
from inside and I held a daughter, the milky night
wrapping us skin to skin. Now those two want
to mother me, bring software and home-baked bread.

Hours with the puzzle of desire, its fierce teeth
in deep as ever and I the same girl. Hard work
thinking about that point where world
and body intersect. Such dissonance. It's autumn
winding down for me, seen from out there.

Great wings of rain along the coast tonight.
Our eucalyptus and blue oaks shake,
let go leaves that slap against the roof.
On my monitor, new growth, geese flying north.
How far away we go to get home.

CELIBACY

Watching the autumn sun set over the swamp
where snipe are flying, I am filled with sadness—
even though I am tonsured.
—Saigyo, in a poem about the shoreline at Oiso

Is there a name for light
that steals inside, breaks through
the sturdiest of locks?
Sun a smudgy vein of red
where the bay touches darkening sky.
Those of us who sleep untended,
who winter over alone,
turn to watch the silent passage,
birds heading south.

TERRITORIES

1.

Born and a blaze of light. Alkali flats. Elko, Nevada.
Nothing gets in the way of the sun.
All day the moan and jangle of freight trains.
Someone photographs your first steps.
Backyard. Grocery store.
A shadow moves along the sidewalk,
jumps when you jump.

2.

Pine and aspen. Wasatch Range.
Great roar of what they call creeks.
Sky the same raw blue but just a slit.
You tip your head back. Granite up there—
cliffs and a jumble of cast-off rocks.
Do places always have their own songs?
You hold your father's hand.

3.

The sky is wrong. There are layers between.
Streaks of gray humidity. *We're transplanted*,
Mother says. A pond to swim in,
the tree house, moss—nothing quite consoles.
One day, six years old, on a bus with your parents,
you shout *It's the Hudson, everybody,*
seeing the bluffs, the only exposed rock around.

4.

The weight of green is what's real now,
all that unfolding, reaching
toward sky—maples, ivy, tended lawns.
In July, you play croquet,
in December, wear matched sweater sets,
read sonnets by Edna St. Vincent Millay:
And last year's leaves are smoke in every lane.

5.

Imperatives of the body—
a bus ride across the Charles to Back Bay,
the borrowed flat, a boy from M.I.T.
who has wanted so long to hold you.
White rug in front of the fireplace.
You feel you're like the city night,
silky and glittering, dark and riverine.

6.

The next lover, older, more confident, takes you
to a desert and to nights, now and then,
when he does not come home.
Small town near a copper mine.
On the map, lakes called *Seco, Mirage*—
just circles of stained sand. Curve of the road,
more saline shore. Invisible bodies.

7.

He wants the Haight. You want the sea,
edge of a continent of longing.
So it's San Francisco, two babies,
milky breasts, your body precious now.
The backyard becomes a refuge for runaways
with their feathers and tambourines.
His lovers are better cooks than you.

8.

Foggiest part of the city—freshwater lake
a block from the sea, a few drenched
eucalyptus trees. Only an occasional sighting
of sunlight. You've taken the two girls,
settled in to *Sesame Street* and *The Love Boat*,
starched ruffles on canopy beds,
long, solitary walks that exhaust you.

9.

Just across a bridge but far enough
for different weather—the first house
you've signed the mortgage for alone.
A roof in need of repair, a water heater to buy,
the half-acre of brambles to clear.
Then the kids help to roll out sod.
Such fierce green alive in a dry land.

10.

Twenty years rooted. Jays come every day,
a barn owl's out there most nights.
Once, a golden eagle in your redwoods.
The kids. Their friends. A ping-pong table.
You hammer things, dig things up, gladly watch
over the roses, seldom look in a mirror,
your body an extension of this place, its servant.

11.

The kids call home from college but the house
is silent otherwise. You go to the mountains
often. Sierra Nevada, roar of wind
through branches, a language before language,
sturdy as a cradle. You feel safe up there,
can follow the visible bones of the landscape—
range and basin, canyon, dome.

12.

Your youngest child is leaving
for Massachusetts, piling books into the trunk
of an old Ford. *There'll be fireflies, and snow!*
This American to and fro. We surrender
to whatever is present, river or empty channel,
red cedar or mountain laurel.
Over and over, dissolved, made new.

SMOKE ALARM

Hearing the story at twenty-five,
I thought it had to do with naiveté,
a newly widowed neighbor
waking to birdsong at midnight,
putting on her slippers and glasses
and climbing up into the attic,
each night looking for a trapped bird,
eager to be on the side of life,
to free the small creature, but finding nothing.

It's two a.m. and I'm wide awake,
fumbling through my own house,
a nine-volt battery in my hand.
And I'm thinking of Mother,
who told that story as we drank iced tea
in a year when everything seemed possible.
Across the continent, Mother is probably awake,
working hard to hold on to a fraction
of what she once knew. She wouldn't remember
how the woman's son finally came,
found a smoke alarm chirping in the rafters.

There is so much we don't get to save,
so much that eludes rescue.
Of course we're not naive, just alone,
the ones who make rituals of bolt locks
and curtains. Noises wake us. Not babies now.
Sometimes mice in the walls or rain in the gutters.
We'll take any chance to make things
make sense. Cries require an answer.

FIRST DAY, ASILOMAR RETREAT

In the din and clatter of this cavernous
state park mess hall, Lyn tells me
she's been listening to Plato's *Republic*
on the tape deck in her car,
reflecting on virtue and the ideal state
from the vantage point of freeways.

We're both past sixty and past the frenzy
of child rearing and parent tending,
past that rush to find a bit of earth,
a garden tangle, a name.
Plato said we'd never emerge
into the full brilliance of the sun,

just live secondhand, aping shadows.
But what are these years for
if not to do the real work,
if not to get it right?
Outside the window, sea birds call.
Waves fall against a fractured shore.

ONE MONTH AT CASA SOTOVENTO

1.

On this cliff above the brittle dance
of wind-blown palms, I look north,
see Kate asleep, the roof beams falling,
glass in that silky hair.
The Hayward fault becomes a mouth
sliding open beneath her bed.

The man running by had said
Huvo un temblor muy grande en California.
Bougainvillea, blood-red
like paper on fire, tangle overhead.

2.

The question is how to let go,
reeducate a body
that braces itself moment to moment
expecting the earth to shift.
Across this bay, beyond the anchored boats,
a lacy reef holds back the sea.

Of course she was safe.
Grown children move in their own orbits.
Let it go. There are enough colors
on one hillside to justify the day.

3.

Last night I dreamed about a husband
thirty years gone, how he loved
women. The ground was not solid
beneath us. Fog swallowed
sidewalks and gardens,
sprawled in the branches of trees.

I write dreams in a green book.
The ceiling fan pushes warm air
in circles and the sea
drags sand across La Ropa Beach.

4.

Setting his wine glass on a rock,
the poet from Seattle
who stayed with Paz in Cuernavaca
says *No need to leave home.*
Just write every day. Poke around
in the rubble. I dare you.

Inland, whole hills are burning.
Charcoal for cooking and ashes for corn.
Smoke, the feathered breast of a bird,
settles onto the bay.

5.

More dreams. Fifty years compressed
in the curve of a shoulder,
office buildings that have no exits,
a teacher's glance, babies mislaid.
What surfaces in the green book
is code. Dark stones

at the headland cup blue fish
in hollows worn by sand.
Stones reach up from a folding continent.
I work with what I can get.

6.

Offshore the breeze is steady.
I float cradled, watching
domed and gentle mountains
rise out of Zihuatanejo Bay.
I recognize those shapes. Lake George.
Pine wind, light on small waves,

Father there and the unmoving
weight of the Adirondacks.
So this is how it is then—
nothing wasted, nothing lost.

METEOR SHOWER

Melody and I flat on our backs
on the hood of the red Toyota, laughing.
We're ready for random light.
Bats sound their way past us.
Frogs chime in from the reeds.
Too early for the main show—
three a.m., they say—but still we search
for streaks, star grit burning
as it falls. We know just looking
counts. Take any excuse for joy.

THROUGH THE LENS, OCTOBER

After a day of torch-bright groves,
sidewalks ankle-deep in fallen leaves,
I walk into a gallery in Stowe,
find the town offered in black and white:
light pearling the limbs of maples;
lawns printed gunmetal gray;
framed roses, unobtrusive in a charcoal hue.
So much reduced to so little.

Everyone needs black and white,
a friend observed decades ago,
so we can get at the bones of things.
I had a darkroom then—
tables hammered together by a lover,
a borrowed enlarger. Late at night,
I stood before the line of trays,
lifting prints with wooden tongs,

trying to transform the lush and complicated
into something manageable, something pure.
How black thrilled me where it pooled
in unlit planes and creases.
True, absolute black. And the white
of exposed paper—a snow field waiting.

But mornings now, I feel my age
and want to be warmed by raw, noisy crimson,
all those greens, jumbled and unframed.
I carry a digital camera. Inside it
encoded in ones and zeroes, Stowe.
Just a blaze of golden light.
The way we get ready for winter.

WAITING TO HEAR ABOUT THE BIOPSY

I sit watching whatever moves:
clouds, a Steller's jay, one strand
of spider web worked free from the branch,
carried through these daylight hours
by its own sheer weightlessness.

CHERNOBYL

Patricia keeps dreaming about cell division.
There are bolts of lightning. Cells clump together,
black and swollen, then, one by one, turn scarlet,
split open like ripe fruit. *It's beautiful,* she says.
Terrifying. Dreams kindled by love for Rina,
a child born somewhere in Russia, orphaned early.

***

I refused to look at the slide when my biopsy
came back yes. The doctor gestured
to his microscope, thinking the shapes would interest me,
as if the mind could be distracted from its dread.
I turned away. And that night, saw ragged edges,
chromosomes with claws and teeth.

***

A student from Kiev wants me to understand
how she felt the day her husband was buried.
She chooses the one verb harsh enough—
opostushonnyi,
to become hollow, to be empty as a desert.
I've been like that for years, she says.
I do not ask what she sees in her dreams.

SHRINE

That was the year of wanting everything back.
I shuffled through the sanctuary
behind men in parkas and Stetson hats,

a woman in a neck brace, restless kids
who fingered the milagros pinned to walls,
the snapshots, abandoned crutches,

testimony to the miraculous
in our own time, even beneath a sky
lashed by jet trails, high tension wires,

even beneath the wilderness of space,
those microwave whispers arriving
from thirteen billion years ago.

It was simpler when Don Bernardo Abeyta
was cured, then built the shrine.
The sky was unbroken then.

It stretched over everything,
mountain range to mountain range,
taut as the indigo cloth on his wife's loom.

I wanted so much to be well,
took my handful of healing dirt
from the carved wooden trough.

FOR WEEKS AFTER THE DIAGNOSIS

I walk beside water,
muscles and joints on autopilot,
nothing at all required from the mind,
which is learning to let go
its harried *now, now, now.*

Ahead of me, women pushing strollers,
old men in running shorts,
each person's body
exquisite, imperfect.
We are witnesses for one another,
partners in the enterprise
of being alive exactly here
where snowy egrets work
the darkness between stones
and herring mill in the shallows.

Most days the sea does no more
than stir pebbles on a narrow beach
but the first morning after a storm,
we're faced with wreckage—
masts, half hulls, splintered decks,
boats torn loose from moorings
west of here, in Sausalito.

The little shiver of gratitude.
Not me. At least
not today.

POISON

Magritte painted a cloud
pushing in through someone's front door,
a seaside cloud, solid as cotton batting

but in miniature. Then he painted
the wooden door's desire to be sky.
He called that scene *poison*

believing the impossible is more
than most people are able to bear.
But it delights us. Every exquisitely

misplaced moon, every torso
half flesh, half oak, every defeat
of gravity delights us.

The gallery is crowded.
A woman, nearly bald,
leans forward to see the cloud.

Though it wasn't expected to work,
she had taken the poison they offered.
What could feel more impossible

than getting herself back after so long?
Perhaps we are born for this,
to be astonished, then go on.